Initial Patterns in Final "iou," "iao" Written Chinese Phonetics

by

Stephen M Kraemer

In the Chinese writing system, many characters are phonetic in nature, i.e., they have a graphic component that indicates the sound or pronunciation of the character. This phonetic component is usually taken from another Chinese character, which exhibits some similarity in pronunciation to the original. Many of these phonetic components are good indicators of sound, i.e., they have the same or nearly the same pronunciation as the original character. However, many phonetic components of characters share only a limited number of phonetic features with the original character.

In this study, a number of Mandarin Chinese characters are listed along with their phonetic character components. The phonetic features that both have in common are also given. In this way, a student or learner of Chinese can see how a character in Mandarin is written phonetically, and what phonetic features or properties are used in its composition.

In addition, the phonetic patterns of pairs or groups of characters that share a Final “iou” or Final “iao” phonetic component are included in this study.

Characters are presented according to which “initial” patterns they illustrate. This includes segments with initial consonants, as well as “zero” or “null” initial segments that begin with the letters “y,” “w,” or “a” in Mandarin.

Compound characters are included whose initial or final pronunciation vary in comparison to their phonetic components. As a result, compound characters that are Totally Perfect or Segment Perfect in comparison to their phonetic components are not included here.

In this study, Mandarin characters are given in pinyin. Characters and their pronunciations are taken from Xinhua Zidian (1971). Where a character is not found in Xinhua Zidian (1971), it is taken from Handian (2004-2015).

Palatal Initial Perfect

敫/激

(jiǎo)/(jī)

敫/憿

(jiǎo)/(jǐ)

丩/叫

(jiū)/(jiào)

九/艽

(jiǔ)/(jiāo)

壳/悫

(qiào)/(què)

秋/锹

(qiū)/(qiāo)

秋/愀

(qiū)/(qiǎo)

肖/屑

(xiāo)/(xiè)

肖/削

(xiāo)/(xuē)

肖/屑

(xiào)/(xiè)

肖/削

(xiào)/(xuē)

Palatal

焦/劁

(jiāo)/(qiāo)

焦/瞧樵谯憔

(jiāo)/(qiáo)

九/仇犰馗艽

(jiǔ)/(qiú)

乔/娇骄

(qiáo)/(jiāo)

乔/矫

(qiáo)/(jiǎo)

乔/峤轿

(qiáo)/(jiào)

秋/湫

(qiū)/(jiǎo)

龟/阄

(qiū)/(jiū)

秋/揪鬏啾

(qiū)/(jiū)

酋/揂

(qiú)/(jiū)

求/救捄

(qiú)/(jiù)

交/洨

(jiāo)/(xiáo)

交/校效

(jiāo)/(xiào)

敫/檄

(jiǎo)/(xí)

九/旭

(jiǔ)/(xù)

孝/教

(xiào)/(jiāo)

孝/教酵

(xiào)/(jiào)

肖/悄

(xiāo)/(qiāo)

肖/悄

(xiāo)/(qiǎo)

肖/俏诮鞘峭

(xiāo)/(qiào)

Voiced Bilabial Initial Perfect

苗/猫

(miáo)/(māo)

苗/猫锚

(miáo)/(máo)

Voiceless Bilabial

票/膘骠镖

(piào)/(biāo)

票/摽鳔

(piào)/(biào)

Voiced Alveolar Initial Perfect

尞/潦

(liáo)/(lǎo)

翏/醪

(liù)/(láo)

翏/寥

(liù)/(liáo)

翏/蓼

(liù)/(liǎo)

翏/廖

(liù)/(liào)

翏/戮

(liù)/(lù)

Voiceless Alveolar
Initial Perfect

条/绦

(tiáo)/(tāo)

Voiceless Alveolar

条/涤

(tiáo)/(dí)

Alveolar

鸟/窎

(niǎo)/(diào)

Palatal/Voiced Alveolar

咎/绺

(jiù)/(liǔ)

㐬/巯

(liú)/(qiú)

翏/璆

(liù)/(qiú)

Palatal/Voiceless Alveolar

秀/透

(xiù)/(tòu)

Palatal/Voiceless Retroflex

敫/缴

(jiǎo)/(zhuó)

九/仇

(jiǔ)/(chóu)

秋/愁

(qiū)/(chóu)

秋/瞅

(qiū)/(chǒu)

秋/甃

(qiū)/(zhòu)

肖/鞘稍捎梢筲
艄蛸
(xiāo)/(shāo)
肖/稍哨
(xiāo)/(shào)
小/少
(xiǎo)/(shǎo)

肖/鞘稍捎梢筲
艄蛸
(xiào)/(shāo)
肖/稍哨
(xiào)/(shào)

Voiced Alveolar/Voiceless Retroflex

㐬/疏梳

(liú)/(shū)

翏/瘳

(liù)/(chōu)

Voiced Alveolar/Voiced Bilabial

翏/缪

(liù)/(miào)

翏/缪谬

(liù)/(miù)

翏/缪

(liù)/(móu)

Palatal/Dental
就/蹴
(jiù)/(cù)

Palatal/Velar

九/旮

(jiǔ)/(gā)

九/轨宄

(jiǔ)/(guǐ)

九/尻

(jiǔ)/(kāo)

咎/晷

(jiù)/(guǐ)

Palatal/y

交/咬

(jiāo)/(yǎo)

敫/邀

(jiǎo)/(yāo)

久/羑

(jiǔ)/(yǒu)

尧/浇

(yáo)/(jiāo)

尧/侥

(yáo)/(jiǎo)

尤/就

(yóu)/(jiù)

酉/酒

(yǒu)/(jiǔ)

酋/猷輶揂

(qiú)/(yóu)

夭/乔

(yāo)/(qiáo)

尧/硗跷

(yáo)/(qiāo)

尧/翘

(yáo)/(qiáo)

尧/翘

(yáo)/(qiào)

酉/酋

(yǒu)/(qiú)

秀/莠

(xiù)/(yǒu)

秀/诱

(xiù)/(yòu)

夭/笑

(yāo)/(xiào)

尧/骁哓

(yáo)/(xiāo)

肴/淆峣

(yáo)/(xiáo)

尧/晓

(yáo)/(xiǎo)

攸/翛

(yōu)/(xiāo)

攸/筱

(yōu)/(xiǎo)

攸/修脩
(yōu)/(xiū)
由/袖岫
(yóu)/(xiù)

Voiced Alveolar/y

旒/毓

(liú)/(yù)

尧/挠铙蛲

(yáo)/(náo)

幼/拗

(yòu)/(niù)

Voiceless Alveolar/y

舀/蹈

(yǎo)/(dǎo)

舀/稻

(yǎo)/(dào)

由/笛迪

(yóu)/(dí)

舀/韬滔
(yǎo)/(tāo)
舀/鞱
(yǎo)/(tǎo)

Voiceless Bilabial/y

肴/驳

(yáo)/(bó)

Voiceless
Retroflex/y
尧/烧
(yáo)/(shāo)
攸/倏
(yōu)/(shū)

由/紬抽
(yóu)/(chōu)
由/紬
(yóu)/(chóu)

繇/繇

(yáo)/(zhòu)

由/轴妯

(yóu)/(zhóu)

由/宙胄

(yóu)/(zhòu)

由/舳

(yóu)/(zhú)

Voiced Retroflex/y

尧/饶娆桡荛

(yáo)/(ráo)

尧/娆绕

(yáo)/(rǎo)

尧/绕

(yáo)/(rào)

尤/扰

(yóu)/(rǎo)

右/若

(yòu)/(ruò)

Velar/y

有/贿

(yǒu)/(huì)

有/贿

(yòu)/(huì)

y

约/哟

(yāo)/(yō)

约/哟

(yāo)/(yo)

夭/饫

(yāo)/(yù)

夭/跃

(yāo)/(yuè)

岳/繇

(yáo)/(yóu)

有/郁

(yǒu)/(yù)

幼/窈

(yòu)/(yǎo)

幼/𩋀

(yòu)/(yào)

有/郁

(yòu)/(yù)

y/a

夭/袄

(yāo)/(ǎo)

夭/岙

(yāo)/(ào)

幼/拗

(yòu)/(ǎo)

幼/拗坳

(yòu)/(ào)

y/w

夭/沃

(yāo)/(wò)

有/洧痏鮪

(yǒu)/(wěi)

References

Cheng, C.C. (1973). *A synchronic phonology of Mandarin Chinese*. The Hague: Mouton.

DeFrancis, John. (1970). *Index volume*. New Haven: Yale University Press.

Handian [<汉典>, '字典']. Online Chinese dictionary. (2004 – 2015). http://www.zdic.net

Kratochvil, Paul. (1968). *The Chinese language today: Features of an emerging standard*. London: Hutchinson & Co., Ltd.

Xinhua zidian (New China dictionary). (1971). Beijing: Shangwu Yinshuguan. [<新华字典>, 1971, 北京：商务印书馆.]

Zhou, Youguang. (1980). *Hanzi shengpang duyin biancha* (A handy look up for the pronunciation of phonetics in Chinese characters). Jilin: Jilin Remnin Chubanshe.
[周 有光, 1980, <汉字声旁读音便查>，吉林：吉林人民出版社.]

Books on the Chinese Writing System by Stephen M. Kraemer

Available on Amazon.com

(www.amazon.com/author/stephenkraemer)

Kraemer, Stephen M. (2017a). *Let's Learn Mandarin Phonics. Seven Basic Phonetic Patterns of Commonly Occurring Chinese Characters.* CreateSpace Independent Publishing Platform.

Kraemer, Stephen M. (2017b). *Let's Learn Mandarin Phonics-2. Final and Final-Tone Perfect Phonetic Patterns of Common Chinese Characters.* CreateSpace Independent Publishing Platform.

Kraemer, Stephen M. (2018a). *Let's Learn Mandarin Phonics-3. Rime Clue, Rime-Tone Clue, Ending Clue, Ending-Tone Clue Phonetic Patterns of Common Chinese Characters.* CreateSpace Independent Publishing Platform.

Kraemer, Stephen M. (2018b). *Let's Learn Mandarin Phonics-4. Initial Clue, Initial-Tone Clue, Tone-Clue and Related Phonetic Patterns of Common Chinese Characters.* CreateSpace Independent Publishing Platform.

Kraemer, Stephen M. (2018c). *Let's Learn Mandarin Phonics-5. Vowel Phonetic Clues for Common Chinese Characters.* CreateSpace Independent Publishing Platform.

Kraemer, Stephen M. (2018d). *Phonetic Clues for Learning Common Chinese Characters.* CreateSpace Independent Publishing Platform.

Kraemer, Stephen M. (2018e). *A Phonetic Guide to Learning Chinese Characters.* CreateSpace Independent Publishing Platform.

Kraemer, Stephen M. (2018f). *Let*'s *Learn Pinyin Final "i" Chinese Characters in Mandarin*. CreateSpace Independent Publishing Platform.

Kraemer, Stephen M. (2018g). *Homorganic Initial Patterns in Common Mandarin Chinese Characters*. CreateSpace Independent Publishing Platform.

Kraemer, Stephen M. (2018h). *Let*'s *Learn Pinyin Final "u/ü" Patterns in Mandarin Chinese Characters*. CreateSpace Independent Publishing Platform.

Kraemer, Stephen M. (2018i). *Coronal Initial Patterns in Common Mandarin Chinese Characters.* CreateSpace Independent Publishing Platform.

Kraemer, Stephen M. (2018j). *Voiceless Alveolar/Retroflex Initial Patterns in Mandarin Chinese Characters*. CreateSpace Independent Publishing Platform.

Kraemer, Stephen M. (2018k). *Velar/Palatal Initial Patterns in Mandarin Chinese Characters*. CreateSpace Independent Publishing Platform.

Kraemer, Stephen M. (2018l). *Pinyin 'an' Rime Patterns in Mandarin Chinese Characters*. CreateSpace Independent Publishing Platform.

Kraemer, Stephen M. (2018m). *Let's Learn Pinyin "n/ng" Ending Patterns in Mandarin Chinese Characters*. CreateSpace Independent Publishing Platform.

Kraemer, Stephen M. (2018n). *Final Patterns in Pinyin "ng" Ending Mandarin Chinese Characters*. CreateSpace Independent Publishing Platform.

Kraemer, Stephen M. (2019). *Initial Perfect and Initial-Tone Perfect Patterns in Mandarin Chinese Characters*. Independent Publishing Platform.

Kraemer, Stephen M. (2019a). *Initial-Rime Perfect and Initial-Ending Perfect Patterns in Mandarin Chinese Characters*. Independent Publishing Platform.

Kraemer, Stephen M. (2019b). *Similar Vowel Patterns in Initial-Perfect Mandarin Chinese Characters.* Independent Publishing Platform.

Kraemer, Stephen M. (2019c). *Homorganic Variation in the Pronunciation of Chinese Characters in Mandarin.* Independent Publishing Platform.

Kraemer, Stephen M. (2019d). *Coronal Variation in the Pronunciation of Chinese Characters in Mandarin.* Independent Publishing Platform.

Kraemer, Stephen M. (2019e). *Pronunciation Variation in V and VC1 Segment Characters in Mandarin.* Independent Publishing Platform.

Kraemer, Stephen M. (2019f). *Dorsal/Coronal Variation in the Pronunciation of Chinese Characters in Mandarin*. Independent Publishing Platform.

Kraemer, Stephen M. (2019g). *A Phonetic Guide to Mandarin Chinese Characters in Color*. Independent Publishing Platform.

Kraemer, Stephen M. (2019h). *Phonetic Clues for Mandarin Chinese Characters in Color*. Independent Publishing Platform.

Kraemer, Stephen M. (2019i). *More Phonetic Clues for Mandarin Chinese Characters in Color*. Independent Publishing Platform.

Kraemer, Stephen M. (2019j). *Even More Phonetic Clues for Mandarin Chinese Characters in Color*. Independent Publishing Platform.

Kraemer, Stephen M. (2019k). *Phonetic Patterns in Mandarin Chinese Characters*. Independent Publishing Platform.

Kraemer, Stephen M. (2019l). *More Phonetic Patterns in Mandarin Chinese Characters*. Independent Publishing Platform.

Kraemer, Stephen M. (2019m). *Even More Phonetic Patterns in Mandarin Chinese Characters*. Independent Publishing Platform.

Kraemer, Stephen M. (2019n). *Still More Phonetic Clues for Mandarin Chinese Characters in Color*. Independent Publishing Platform.

Kraemer, Stephen M. (2019o). *More and More Phonetic Clues for Mandarin Chinese Characters in Color*. Independent Publishing Platform.

Kraemer, Stephen M. (2019p). *Still More Phonetic Patterns in Mandarin Chinese Characters*. Independent Publishing Platform.

Kraemer, Stephen M. (2019q). *A Phonetic Color Guide to Mandarin Chinese Characters*. Independent Publishing Platform.

Kraemer, Stephen M. (2019r).
Pinyin "ch/c" Initial Patterns in Mandarin Chinese Characters. Independent Publishing Platform.

Kraemer, Stephen M. (2019s).
Pinyin "zh/z" Initial Patterns in Mandarin Chinese Characters. Independent Publishing Platform.

Kraemer, Stephen M. (2019t).
Pinyin "sh/s" Initial Patterns in Mandarin Chinese Characters. Independent Publishing Platform.

Kraemer, Stephen M. (2019u).
Pinyin "sh/x" Initial Patterns in Mandarin Chinese Characters. Independent Publishing Platform.

Kraemer, Stephen M. (2019v). *Pinyin "zh/j" Initial Patterns in Mandarin Chinese Characters*. Independent Publishing Platform.

Kraemer, Stephen M. (2019w). *Pinyin "z/c" Initial Patterns in Mandarin Chinese Characters*. Independent Publishing Platform.

Kraemer, Stephen M. (2019x). *Dental Initial Patterns in Mandarin Chinese Characters*. Independent Publishing Platform.

Kraemer, Stephen M. (2019y). *Dental/Palatal Initial Patterns in Mandarin Chinese Characters*. Independent Publishing Platform.

Kraemer, Stephen M. (2019z). *Retroflex/Palatal Initial Patterns in Mandarin Chinese Characters*. Independent Publishing Platform.

Kraemer, Stephen M. (2019aa). *Final Patterns in Velar/Palatal Mandarin Chinese Characters*. Independent Publishing Platform.

Kraemer, Stephen M. (2019ab). *Pinyin "e/i" Single Vowel Patterns in Mandarin Chinese Characters*. Independent Publishing Platform.

Kraemer, Stephen M. (2019ac). *Pinyin "a/e" Single Vowel Patterns in Mandarin Chinese Characters*. Independent Publishing Platform.

Kraemer, Stephen M. (2019ad). *Retroflex/Dental Initial Patterns in Mandarin Chinese Characters*. Independent Publishing Platform.

Kraemer, Stephen M. (2019ae). *Pinyin "ch/sh" Initial Patterns in Mandarin Chinese Characters*. Independent Publishing Platform.

Kraemer, Stephen M. (2019af). *Pinyin "zh/sh" Initial Patterns in Mandarin Chinese Characters*. Independent Publishing Platform.

Kraemer, Stephen M. (2019ag). *Pinyin "zh/ch" Initial Patterns in Mandarin Chinese Characters*. Independent Publishing Platform.

Kraemer, Stephen M. (2019ah). *Retroflex Initial Patterns in Mandarin Chinese Characters*. Independent Publishing Platform.

Kraemer, Stephen M. (2019ai). *Palatal/ "l" Initial Patterns in Mandarin Chinese Characters*. Independent Publishing Platform.

Kraemer, Stephen M. (2019aj). *Alveolar/Palatal Initial Patterns in Mandarin Chinese Characters*. Independent Publishing Platform.

Kraemer, Stephen M. (2019ak). *Retroflex/Voiced Alveolar Initial Patterns in Mandarin Chinese Characters*. Independent Publishing Platform.

Kraemer, Stephen M. (2019al). *Pinyin "y" Patterns in Mandarin Chinese Characters*. Independent Publishing Platform.

Kraemer, Stephen M. (2019am). *Pinyin "w" and "w/y" Patterns in Mandarin Chinese Characters*. Independent Publishing Platform.

Kraemer, Stephen M. (2019an). *V Segment Patterns in Mandarin Chinese Characters*. Independent Publishing Platform.

Kraemer, Stephen M. (2019ao). *Pinyin "ai/i" Vowel Patterns in Mandarin Chinese Characters*. Independent Publishing Platform.

Kraemer, Stephen M. (2019ap). *Phonetic Patterns in Mandarin Chinese Characters: Pinyin "a" Finals and Unrounded Diphthongs*. Independent Publishing Platform.

Kraemer, Stephen M. (2019aq). *Phonetic Patterns in Mandarin Chinese Characters: Pinyin "e" Finals and Unrounded Diphthongs*. Independent Publishing Platform.

Kraemer, Stephen M. (2019ar). *Phonetic Patterns in Mandarin Chinese Characters: Unrounded Diphthong Finals*. Independent Publishing Platform.

Kraemer, Stephen M. (2019as). *Phonetic Patterns in Mandarin Chinese Characters: Rounded Medial Vowels in V Finals*. Independent Publishing Platform.

Kraemer, Stephen M. (2019at). *Phonetic Patterns in Mandarin Chinese Characters: Rounded Medial and Rounded Ending Vowels in V Finals*. Independent Publishing Platform.

Kraemer, Stephen M. (2019au). *Phonetic Patterns in Mandarin Chinese Characters: Pinyin "u" and Rounded Medial Vowels in V Finals*. Independent Publishing Platform.

Kraemer, Stephen M. (2019av). *Phonetic Patterns of Chinese Characters: Velar / "w" and Velar / "y" in Mandarin*. Independent Publishing Platform.

Kraemer, Stephen M. (2019aw). *Phonetic Patterns of Chinese Characters: Alveolar / "y" in Mandarin*. Independent Publishing Platform.

Kraemer, Stephen M. (2019ax). *Phonetic Patterns of Chinese Characters: Retroflex / "y" in Mandarin*. Independent Publishing Platform.

Kraemer, Stephen M. (2019ay). *Phonetic Patterns of Chinese Characters: Palatal / "y" in Mandarin*. Independent Publishing Platform.

Kraemer, Stephen M. (2019az). *Phonetic Patterns of Chinese Characters: Pinyin "g/k" in Mandarin*. Independent Publishing Platform.

Kraemer, Stephen M. (2019aaa). *Phonetic Patterns of Chinese Characters: Pinyin "g/h" in Mandarin*. Independent Publishing Platform.

Kraemer, Stephen M. (2019aab). *Phonetic Patterns of Chinese Characters: Pinyin "h/k" in Mandarin*. Independent Publishing Platform.

Kraemer, Stephen M. (2019aac). *Phonetic Patterns of Chinese Characters: Velar Initials in Mandarin*. Independent Publishing Platform.

Kraemer, Stephen M. (2019aad). *Phonetic Patterns in Mandarin Chinese Characters: Pinyin "i/ie" Finals*. Independent Publishing Platform.

Kraemer, Stephen M. (2019aae). *Phonetic Patterns in Mandarin Chinese Characters: Pinyin "i/a" and "i/ei" Finals*. Independent Publishing Platform.

Kraemer, Stephen M. (2019aaf). *Phonetic Patterns of Chinese Characters: Pinyin "d/t" Initials in Mandarin*. Independent Publishing Platform.

Kraemer, Stephen M. (2019aag). *Phonetic Patterns of Chinese Characters: Alveolar Initials in Mandarin*. Independent Publishing Platform.

Kraemer, Stephen M. (2019aah). *Phonetic Patterns of Chinese Characters: Pinyin "b/p" Initials in Mandarin*. Independent Publishing Platform.

Kraemer, Stephen M. (2019aai). *Phonetic Patterns of Chinese Characters: Pinyin "f/b" and "f/p" Initials in Mandarin*. Independent Publishing Platform.

Kraemer, Stephen M. (2019aaj). *Phonetic Patterns of Chinese Characters: Labial Initials in Mandarin*. Independent Publishing Platform.

Kraemer, Stephen M. (2019aak). *Phonetic Patterns in Mandarin Chinese Characters: Pinyin "uo" and Unrounded V Finals*. Independent Publishing Platform.

Kraemer, Stephen M. (2019aal). *Phonetic Patterns in Mandarin Chinese Characters: Pinyin "u" and Unrounded V Finals*. Independent Publishing Platform.

Kraemer, Stephen M.(2019aam). *Phonetic Patterns in Mandarin Chinese Characters: Pinyin "u" and Rounded Ending Vowels in V Finals*. Independent Publishing Platform.

Kraemer, Stephen M.(2019aan). *Phonetic Patterns in Mandarin Chinese Characters: Rounded Ending Vowels in V Finals*. Independent Publishing Platform.

Kraemer, Stephen M.(2019aao). *Phonetic Patterns in Mandarin Chinese Characters: Pinyin "an"/"en"/"in" Finals*. Independent Publishing Platform.

Kraemer, Stephen M.(2019aap). *Phonetic Patterns in Mandarin Chinese Characters: V/VC1 Finals with a Rounded Vowel*. Independent Publishing Platform.

Kraemer, Stephen M.(2019aaq). *Phonetic Patterns in Mandarin Chinese Characters: V Finals with a Rounded Vowel Plus VC1 Finals with Unrounded V*. Independent Publishing Platform.

Kraemer, Stephen M.(2019aar). *Phonetic Patterns in Mandarin Chinese Characters: V/VC1 Finals with Unrounded Vowels*. Independent Publishing Platform.

Kraemer, Stephen M.(2019aas). *Phonetic Patterns in Mandarin Chinese Characters: Pinyin "n" Ending Finals with One Rounded Vowel*. Independent Publishing Platform.

Kraemer, Stephen M.(2019aat). *Phonetic Patterns in Mandarin Chinese Characters: VC1 Finals with One Rounded Vowel*. Independent Publishing Platform.

Kraemer, Stephen M.(2019aau). *Phonetic Patterns in Mandarin Chinese Characters: Pinyin "n" Ending Finals with Rounded and Unrounded Vowels*. Independent Publishing Platform.

Kraemer, Stephen M.(2019aav). *Phonetic Patterns in Mandarin Chinese Characters: VC1 Finals with Rounded and Unrounded Vowels*. Independent Publishing Platform.

Kraemer, Stephen M.(2020). *Phonetic Patterns in Mandarin Chinese Characters: Pinyin "ng" Ending Finals with Unrounded Vowels*. Independent Publishing Platform.

Kraemer, Stephen M.(2020a). *Phonetic Patterns in Mandarin Chinese Characters: Pinyin "n/ng" Ending Finals with Unrounded Vowels*. Independent Publishing Platform.

Kraemer, Stephen M.(2020b). *Phonetic Patterns in Mandarin Chinese Characters: V/VC1 Finals*. Independent Publishing Platform.

Kraemer, Stephen M.(2020c). *Phonetic Patterns in Mandarin Chinese Characters: VC1 Finals with Unrounded Vowels*. Independent Publishing Platform.

Kraemer, Stephen M.(2020d). *Phonetic Patterns in Mandarin Chinese Characters: V Finals with a Rounded Medial Vowel Plus Unrounded V*. Independent Publishing Platform.

Kraemer, Stephen M.(2020e). *Phonetic Patterns in Mandarin Chinese Characters: V Finals with a Rounded Ending Vowel Plus Unrounded V*. Independent Publishing Platform.

Kraemer, Stephen M.(2020f). *Phonetic Patterns in Mandarin Chinese Characters: Labial/Velar Initials and Pinyin "m"/"w"*. Independent Publishing Platform.

Kraemer, Stephen M.(2020g). *Phonetic Patterns in Mandarin Chinese Characters: Velar/Retroflex Initials*. Independent Publishing Platform.

Kraemer, Stephen M.(2020h). *Phonetic Patterns in Mandarin Chinese Characters: Velar/Alveolar Initials*. Independent Publishing Platform.

Kraemer, Stephen M.(2020i). *Phonetic Patterns in Mandarin Chinese Characters: Palatal Initials*. Independent Publishing Platform.

Kraemer, Stephen M.(2020j). *Phonetic Patterns in Chinese Characters: Pinyin "a/e" Variation in Mandarin*. Independent Publishing Platform.

Kraemer, Stephen M.(2020k). *Phonetic Groups in Chinese Characters: All Unrounded Vowel Finals in Mandarin*. Independent Publishing Platform.

Kraemer, Stephen M.(2020l). *Phonetic Groups in Chinese Characters: All Unrounded Vowel Finals in Mandarin Volume 2*. Independent Publishing Platform.

Kraemer, Stephen M.(2020m). *Phonetic Groups in Chinese Characters: All Unrounded Vowel Finals in Mandarin Volume 3*. Independent Publishing Platform.

Kraemer, Stephen M.(2020n). *Phonetic Groups in Chinese Characters: All Vowel Finals in Mandarin*. Independent Publishing Platform.

Kraemer, Stephen M.(2020o). *Phonetic Groups in Chinese Characters: All Vowel Finals in Mandarin Volume 2*. Independent Publishing Platform.

Kraemer, Stephen M.(2020p). *Phonetic Groups in Chinese Characters: All Vowel Finals in Mandarin Volume 3*. Independent Publishing Platform.

Kraemer, Stephen M.(2020q). *Phonetic Patterns in Mandarin Chinese Characters: Final Perfect with Palatal j/x, q/x Initials*. Independent Publishing Platform.

Kraemer, Stephen M.(2020r). *Phonetic Groups in Chinese Characters: All Unrounded Vowel Finals in Mandarin Volume 4*. Independent Publishing Platform.

Kraemer, Stephen M.(2020s). *Phonetic Groups in Chinese Characters: All Vowel Finals in Mandarin Volume 4*. Independent Publishing Platform.

Kraemer, Stephen M.(2020t). *Phonetic Patterns in Mandarin Chinese Characters: Final Perfect with Palatal j/q Initials*. Independent Publishing Platform.

Kraemer, Stephen M.(2020u). *Phonetic Patterns in Mandarin Chinese Characters: Final Perfect with Palatal Initials*. Independent Publishing Platform.

Kraemer, Stephen M.(2020v). *Phonetic Components for Meaning in Mandarin Chinese Characters*. Independent Publishing Platform.

Kraemer, Stephen M.(2020w). *Phonetic Components for Meaning in Mandarin Chinese Characters Volume 2*. Independent Publishing Platform.

Kraemer, Stephen M.(2020x). *Phonetic Components for Meaning in Mandarin Chinese Characters Volume 3*. Independent Publishing Platform.

Kraemer, Stephen M.(2020y). *Phonetic Components for Meaning in Mandarin Chinese Characters Volume 4*. Independent Publishing Platform.

Kraemer, Stephen M.(2020z). *Phonetic Components for Meaning in Mandarin Chinese Characters Volume 5*. Independent Publishing Platform.

Kraemer, Stephen M.(2020aa). *Phonetic Components for Meaning in Mandarin Chinese Characters Volume 6*. Independent Publishing Platform.

Kraemer, Stephen M.(2020ab). *Phonetic Components for Meaning in Mandarin Chinese Characters Volume 7*. Independent Publishing Platform.

Kraemer, Stephen M.(2020ac). *Semantic Compounds in Mandarin Chinese Characters*. Independent Publishing Platform.

Kraemer, Stephen M.(2020ad). *Patterns and Formulas for Phonetic Groups in Mandarin Chinese Characters*. Independent Publishing Platform.

Kraemer, Stephen M.
(2020ae-ah).
Patterns and Formulas for Phonetic Groups in Mandarin Chinese Characters Volume 2-5.
Independent Publishing Platform.

Kraemer, Stephen M.
(2020ai-al).
Patterns and Formulas for Phonetic Groups in Mandarin Chinese Characters Volume 6-9.
Independent Publishing Platform.

Kraemer, Stephen M.
(2020am-ap).
Patterns and Formulas for Phonetic Groups in Mandarin Chinese Characters Volume 10-12, 14. Independent Publishing Platform.

Kraemer, Stephen M.
(2020aq-at).
Patterns and Formulas for Phonetic Groups in Mandarin Chinese Characters Volume 15-18.
Independent Publishing Platform.

Kraemer, Stephen M.
(2020au-ax).
Patterns and Formulas for Phonetic Groups in Mandarin Chinese Characters Volume 19-22.
Independent Publishing Platform.

Kraemer, Stephen M.
(2020ay-aab).
Patterns and Formulas for Phonetic Groups in Mandarin Chinese Characters Volume 23-26.
Independent Publishing Platform.

Kraemer, Stephen M.
(2020aac-aaf).
Patterns and Formulas for Phonetic Groups in Mandarin Chinese Characters Volume 27-30.
Independent Publishing Platform.

Kraemer, Stephen M.
(2020aag-aaj).
Patterns and Formulas for Phonetic Groups in Mandarin Chinese Characters Volume 31-34.
Independent Publishing Platform.

Kraemer, Stephen M.
(2020aak-aan).
Patterns and Formulas for Phonetic Groups in Mandarin Chinese Characters Volume 35-38.
Independent Publishing Platform.

Kraemer, Stephen M.
(2020aao-aar).
Patterns and Formulas for Phonetic Groups in Mandarin Chinese Characters Volume 39-42.
Independent Publishing Platform.

Kraemer, Stephen M.
(2020aas-aav).
Patterns and Formulas for Phonetic Groups in Mandarin Chinese Characters Volume 43-46.
Independent Publishing Platform.

Kraemer, Stephen M.
(2020aaw-aaz).
Patterns and Formulas for Phonetic Groups in Mandarin Chinese Characters Volume 47-50.
Independent Publishing Platform.

Kraemer, Stephen M.
(2020aaaa-aaad).
Patterns and Formulas for Phonetic Groups in Mandarin Chinese Characters Volume 51-54.
Independent Publishing Platform.

Kraemer, Stephen M.
(2020aaae-aaah).
Patterns and Formulas for Phonetic Groups in Mandarin Chinese Characters Volume 55-58.
Independent Publishing Platform

Kraemer, Stephen M.(2021).
Patterns and Formulas for Phonetic Groups in Mandarin Chinese Characters Volume 58.
Independent Publishing Platform.

Kraemer, Stephen M.(2021a-d). *Patterns and Formulas for Phonetic Groups in Mandarin Chinese Characters Volume 59-62.* Independent Publishing Platform.

Kraemer, Stephen M.(2021e-f). *Patterns and Formulas for Phonetic Groups in Mandarin Chinese Characters Volume 63-64.* Independent Publishing Platform.

Kraemer, Stephen M.(2021g). *Homographic Components in Homophonous Mandarin Characters*. Independent Publishing Platform.

Kraemer, Stephen M.(2021h). *Homographic Components in Homophonous Mandarin Characters Volume 2.* Independent Publishing Platform.

Kraemer, Stephen M.(2021i). *Homophonous Characters with Two Components in Mandarin*. Independent Publishing Platform.

Kraemer, Stephen M.(2021j). *Homophonous Characters with Two Homographic Components in Mandarin*. Independent Publishing Platform.

Kraemer, Stephen M.(2021k). *Homophonous Characters with Two Components in Mandarin Volume 2*. Independent Publishing Platform.

Kraemer, Stephen M.(2021l). *Phonetic Patterns in Homophonous Mandarin Characters*. Independent Publishing Platform.

Kraemer, Stephen M.(2021m-p). *Phonetic Patterns in Homophonous Mandarin Characters Volume 2-5.* Independent Publishing Platform.

Kraemer, Stephen M.(2021q). *Phonetic Patterns in Homophonous Mandarin Characters Volume 6.* Independent Publishing Platform.

Kraemer, Stephen M.(2021r). *Phonetic Patterns in Homophonous Mandarin Characters Volume 7.* Independent Publishing Platform.

Kraemer, Stephen M.(2021s). *Phonetic Patterns in Homophonous Mandarin Characters Volume 8.* Independent Publishing Platform.

Kraemer, Stephen M.(2021t). *Phonetic Patterns in Homophonous Mandarin Characters Volume 9.* Independent Publishing Platform.

Kraemer, Stephen M.(2021u). *Phonetic Patterns in Homophonous Mandarin Characters Volume 10.* Independent Publishing Platform.

Kraemer, Stephen M.(2021v). *Phonetic Patterns in Homophonous Mandarin Characters Volume 10.* Independent Publishing Platform.

Kraemer, Stephen M.(2021w). *Phonetic Patterns in Homophonous Mandarin Characters Volume 11.* Independent Publishing Platform.

Kraemer, Stephen M.(2021x). *Phonetic Patterns in Homophonous Mandarin Characters Volume 12*. Independent Publishing Platform.

Kraemer, Stephen M.(2021y). *Phonetic Properties of Common Chinese Characters in Mandarin*. Independent Publishing Platform.

Kraemer, Stephen M.(2021z). *Phonetic Properties of Common Chinese Characters in Mandarin Volume 2*. Independent Publishing Platform.

Kraemer, Stephen M.(2021aa). *Phonetic Properties of Common Chinese Characters in Mandarin Volume 3*. Independent Publishing Platform.

Kraemer, Stephen M.(2021ab). *Learn Chinese Characters through Sound and Meaning*. Independent Publishing Platform.

Kraemer, Stephen M.(2021ac). *Learn Chinese Characters through Sound and Meaning Volume 2*. Independent Publishing Platform.

Kraemer, Stephen M.(2021ad). *Learn Chinese Characters through Sound and Meaning Volume 3*. Independent Publishing Platform.

Kraemer, Stephen M.(2021ae). *Learn Chinese Characters through Sound and Meaning Volume 4*. Independent Publishing Platform.

Kraemer, Stephen M.(2021af). *Learn Chinese Characters through Sound and Meaning Volume 5*. Independent Publishing Platform.

Kraemer, Stephen M.(2021ag). *Common Phonetic Chinese Characters in Color*. Independent Publishing Platform.

Kraemer, Stephen M.(2021ah). *Common Phonetic Chinese Characters Traditional and Simplified.* Independent Publishing Platform.

Kraemer, Stephen M.(2021ai). *Phonetic Chinese Characters Traditional and Simplified.* Independent Publishing Platform.

Kraemer, Stephen M.(2021aj). *Phonetic Chinese Characters Traditional and Simplified Volume* 2. Independent Publishing Platform.

Kraemer, Stephen M.(2021ak). *Phonetic Regularity in Traditional Versus Simplified Chinese Characters*. Independent Publishing Platform.

Kraemer, Stephen M.(2021al). *Phonetic Regularity in Traditional Versus Simplified Chinese Characters Volume 2.* Independent Publishing Platform.

Kraemer, Stephen M.(2021am). *Phonetic Regularity in Traditional Versus Simplified Chinese Characters Volume 3.* Independent Publishing Platform.

Kraemer, Stephen M.(2021an). *Phonetic Regularity in Traditional Versus Simplified Chinese Characters Volume 4.* Independent Publishing Platform.

Kraemer, Stephen M.(2021ao). *Phonetic Regularity in Traditional Versus Simplified Chinese Characters Volume 5.* Independent Publishing Platform.

Kraemer, Stephen M.(2021ap). *Phonetic Regularity in Traditional Versus Simplified Chinese Characters Volume 6.* Independent Publishing Platform.

Kraemer, Stephen M.(2021aq). *Phonetic Regularity in Traditional Versus Simplified Chinese Characters Volume 7.* Independent Publishing Platform.

Kraemer, Stephen M.(2021ar). *Phonetic Regularity in Traditional Versus Simplified Chinese Characters Volume 8.* Independent Publishing Platform.

Kraemer, Stephen M.(2021as). *Phonetic Regularity in Traditional Versus Simplified Chinese Characters Volume 9.* Independent Publishing Platform.

Kraemer, Stephen M.(2022). *Phonetic Regularity in Traditional Versus Simplified Chinese Characters Volume 10.* Independent Publishing Platform.

Kraemer, Stephen M.(2022a). *Phonetic Regularity of Similar Form Characters in Mandarin.* Independent Publishing Platform.

Kraemer, Stephen M.(2022b). *Phonetic Regularity of Similar Form Characters in Mandarin Volume 2.* Independent Publishing Platform.

Kraemer, Stephen M.(2022c). *Phonetic Regularity of Homophonous Phonetics in Chinese Writing.* Independent Publishing Platform.

Kraemer, Stephen M.(2022d). *Phonetic Regularity of Homophonous Phonetics in Chinese Writing Volume 2.* Independent Publishing Platform.

Kraemer, Stephen M.(2022e). *Phonetic Regularity of Homophonous Phonetics in Chinese Writing Volume 2.* Independent Publishing Platform.

Kraemer, Stephen M.(2022f). *Phonetic Regularity of Same Segment Phonetics in Chinese Writing.* Independent Publishing Platform.

Kraemer, Stephen M.(2022g). *Phonetic Regularity of Same Segment Phonetics in Chinese Writing Volume 2.* Independent Publishing Platform.

Kraemer, Stephen M.(2022h). *Phonetic Patterns of "Shi" Phonetics in Chinese Writing*. Independent Publishing Platform.

Kraemer, Stephen M.(2022i). *Palatal "i" Phonetics in Chinese Writing.* Independent Publishing Platform.

Kraemer, Stephen M.(2022j). *Dental "i" Phonetics in Chinese Writing.* Independent Publishing Platform.

Kraemer, Stephen M.(2022k).
Alveolar "i" Phonetics in Chinese Writing.
Independent Publishing Platform.

Kraemer, Stephen M.(2022l).
Coronal "e" Phonetics in Chinese Writing.
Independent Publishing Platform.

Kraemer, Stephen M.(2022m).
Coronal "ai" Phonetics in Chinese Writing.
Independent Publishing Platform.

Kraemer, Stephen M.(2022n).
Retroflex "i" Phonetics in Chinese Writing.
Independent Publishing Platform.

Kraemer, Stephen M.(2022o).
Coronal "a" Phonetics in Chinese Writing.
Independent Publishing Platform.

Kraemer, Stephen M.(2022p).
Final "ie" Phonetics in Chinese Writing.
Independent Publishing Platform.

Kraemer, Stephen M.(2022q). *"Yi" Phonetics in Chinese Writing*. Independent Publishing Platform.

Kraemer, Stephen M.(2022r). *A Phonetic Guide to Learning Chinese Characters Volume* 2. Independent Publishing Platform.

Kraemer, Stephen M.(2022s). *Coronal "i" Phonetic Characters in Mandarin Chinese.* Independent Publishing Platform.

Kraemer, Stephen M.(2022t). *Pronunciation Variation in Final "i" Mandarin Chinese Characters.* Independent Publishing Platform.

Kraemer, Stephen M.(2022u). *Unrounded Vowel Finals in Alternate Pronunciation of Mandarin Characters.* Independent Publishing Platform.

Kraemer, Stephen M.(2022v). *Rounded Vowel Finals in Alternate Pronunciation of Mandarin Characters.* Independent Publishing Platform.

Kraemer, Stephen M.(2022w). *VC Finals in Alternate Pronunciation of Mandarin Characters.* Independent Publishing Platform.

Kraemer, Stephen M.(2022x). *Final "ao" Phonetics in Chinese Writing.* Independent Publishing Platform.

Kraemer, Stephen M.(2022y). *Final "uo" Phonetics in Chinese Writing.* Independent Publishing Platform.

Kraemer, Stephen M.(2022z). *Final "ou" Phonetics in Chinese Writing.* Independent Publishing Platform.

Kraemer, Stephen M.(2022aa). *Final "u" Phonetics in Chinese Writing*. Independent Publishing Platform.

Kraemer, Stephen M.(2022ab). *Final "iao" Phonetics in Chinese Writing*. Independent Publishing Platform.

Kraemer, Stephen M.(2022ac). *Final "uei" and "uai" Phonetics in Chinese Writing*. Independent Publishing Platform.

Kraemer, Stephen M.(2022ad). *Coronal "u" [u] Phonetics in Chinese Writing*. Independent Publishing Platform.

Kraemer, Stephen M.(2022ae). *Chinese Phonetic Characters with All Back, Rounded Vowel Finals*. Independent Publishing Platform.

www.ingramcontent.com/pod-product-compliance
Lightning Source LLC
LaVergne TN
LVHW010113170826
845678LV00012B/2389

* 9 7 9 8 3 6 6 7 0 5 7 1 4 *